This
MW00893310
Belongs To:

Journals to write in

Positive Party Publishing

SUGAR LAND, TEXAS

Made in the USA
Monee, IL
16 September 2021

78241561R10073